JAMES DETHERIDGE

LIFE, LOVE & WAR

LIFE, LOVE & WAR

Stratton Press, LLC
1603 Capitol Ave, Suite 310,
Cheyenne, WY 82001
www.stratton-press.com
1-888-323-7009

ISBN (Paperback): 978-1-64345-282-1
ISBN (Ebook): 978-1-64345-281-4

Printed in the United States of America

A United States veteran who had served the American people and our great country through his service in the Marine Reserves, US Army, US Air Force during the Vietnam War.

Be happy, young man, in thy youth.
Be sad, young man, when you fight a war, and learn the truth.

—Bob Detheridge, Vietnam Veteran
Served 1966–1967

In the last great invasion, of the last great war; the greatest danger for eight men...was saving one.

—*Saving Private Ryan*

Foreword

James Robert Detheridge is my brother, whom I am very proud of. His life has not been easy; however, he has not only succeeded but has also excelled in every endeavor he has attempted. As I typed my brother's memoirs, I read about things he experienced in Vietnam that I was not aware of. I cannot even begin to imagine going through what my brother has endured. Those of us who enjoy the freedom of America need to realize the astronomical price our military has paid and continues to pay through their posttraumatic memories and fears, as well as the price their families endure. America would not be free without these men and women who have paid for our freedom with their very lives. My brother is a man of principle, discipline, and passion. His life reflects many Americans, especially those who have served in the military. He is a man that I admire, respect, and love very much.

—Carolyn Gunn, 2006

ACKNOWLEDGMENTS

I want to thank my sister, Carolyn, for helping me from start to finish on this autobiography. It was my idea, but she encouraged me to begin this work; and without her, this autobiography would never exist. Thanks again, sister, and God bless. You are the best sister a man could ever have.

Eventhough the word "If" is little, it is used so often in the context of "If this hadn't happened or if I hadn't done that, everything would have been okay or better. So the little word "If" is a very important word in describing things that could have been.

—James R. Detheridge, USMCR Permanent Corporal
(Reg) US Army Specialist 4 (E-4),
(Reg) US Air Force TSgt,
(E-6) Vietnam Veteran IV Corps 1966–1967

LIFE

Who am I, and why would I write about my life? The answer to this question is that I am a nobody and also everybody!

I am just a common, ordinary man like most Americans. The only thing that makes me different is my military service in the Vietnam War, which caused traumatic changes in me and every other veteran who had seen combat action and war up close. I did not ask to be born, but I have made the best of my life's ups and downs.

I was born to my mother, Esther Huffine-Detheridge (maiden name), and father, Charles Edward Detheridge, at 5:30 a.m. on February 21, 1935. It was a cold and rainy morning at the Louisville General Hospital in Louisville, Kentucky. Louisville General Hospital was for people who had no money or, for that matter, even a roof over their head during the Great Depression. You may wonder how I knew that the day I was born was a cold and rainy day. The answer is I have always loved to watch the rain, so one day I asked my mother why I loved the rain so much, and she replied, "It is probably because the day you were born, it rained all day, and it had rained for weeks before your birth."

My earliest memory is of watching a large white house floating down the Ohio River during the flood of 1937. The next thing I remember is living with my aunt Clara and uncle Goble in Woodrow, Kentucky. Aunt Clara was my father's sister. She took care of me in the hills of Kentucky because my mother was in Louisville trying to work and survive following her separation and divorce from my father. My aunt Clara was a wonderful person, and so was my uncle Gobel, who taught me how to hunt and survive in the hills of Kentucky. My aunt Clara was not only a wonderful person but also probably the best cook that I have ever known. Every morning she would make her delicious homemade biscuits, fried ham, red-eye gravy, and the most delicious fried eggs. She also made milk gravy that tasted so good over her biscuits. I remember when I first went to live with my aunt and uncle, I loved her biscuits so much that every morning I would ask her to make "bikuts." You see, I couldn't pronounce "biscuits," but I wanted to be sure she made those "bikuts."

I will never forget visiting my aunt and uncle one very cold winter. I had gone rabbit hunting and was returning to the farmhouse with the three rabbits I had killed, which we would have that evening for supper, when I decided to take a shortcut across a frozen pond. Well, about halfway across, the ice started cracking from my weight, and I fell through the ice. I was in ice-cold water up to my neck, but I managed to break the ice with my shotgun until I got to dry land, and then I walked three miles to the farmhouse. I managed to bring the rabbits with me, which tasted delicious for supper, along with my aunt Clara's famous biscuits. It took me a few days to really thaw out and get some warmth back into my body. I didn't even get a cold. Oh well, that is the positive thing of being young, I guess, thinking and almost being immortal.

On one occasion, I saw five or six fox squirrels in a tree by the farmhouse and went to get my uncle's shotgun. When I found it, I loaded it and fired at the squirrels. Much to my surprise, I was knocked down the side of the hill by the kick of the ten-gauge shotgun. After picking myself up in the creek at the bottom of the hill, I realized that little boys my age should never shoot a ten-gauge shotgun, especially when both barrels fire at the same time. My uncle Gobel taught me the fine art of Kentucky windage and expert marksmanship. Little did he know at the time how handy this would be in keeping me alive later, in 1966–1967, during the Vietnam War. Even after I left my Kentucky mountain home, where I lived some of the most enjoyable times of my life, I visited them every summer when school was out. One summer, when I was about twelve years old, I was visiting with my aunt and uncle when I decided to take our coonhounds and go for a night hunt. After I was through hunting, I was walking home with the hound dogs, and I had to go through a graveyard. I heard a loud moaning sound and looked toward the sound, where I saw a white ghost-like thing rising from behind a tombstone. Even then, I wasn't afraid of anything, so I took a few shots at it with my .22 rifle, when I heard my uncle Gobel scream, "Don't shoot, Bobby. It's me!" My uncle had a white sheet over his head, trying to scare me, but it almost got him killed, and I almost lost my beloved uncle Gobel.

During that same summer, I was sitting under an old hickory tree, waiting for a fox squirrel to come out of its nest, when I heard rifle fire and saw bullets kicking up around my feet. I peeked around the tree and saw this guy shooting at me, so I returned fire and shot about fifteen .22 bullets at him before he took off running. It is unbelievable that I had my first combat firefight at the age of twelve.

Every summer, when I visited my aunt and uncle, we would hitch up our two mules to the farm wagon and take a trip to Custer, Kentucky, where the half-brother of my uncle Gobel, Shang Lucas, lived with his family. I always had a wonderful time when we visited with the Lucas family. I guess it was partly because he had a daughter named Wilma Lee Lucas. She was the first girl who taught me to play the game spin the bottle and who was the first girl that I ever kissed. Years later, I went back to Custer, Kentucky, but did not find Shang or Wilma Lee Lucas.

My uncle Gobel and aunt Clara were sharecroppers and worked a farm in Woodrow, Kentucky, owned by Raymond Drain. My uncle had an acre of tobacco base and also raised corn and alfalfa to feed his milk cows. In those days, during the Great Depression, a sharecropper lived on credit in order to buy the necessities of life, and then when his farm crops were sold in the fall of the year, the farmer would pay his debts he had accumulated during the crop-growing season. If the sharecropper had a good year, he would get a higher part of the cash crop and would have some money left over; but if it was a bad year, because of the weather, he would most likely not be able to pay his debt and start out in the hole for the next year. My uncle had hogs, which he butchered himself, and he had a homemade smokehouse in which he cured the smoked hams with hickory wood he burned in the smokehouse.

My aunt Clara had a large garden in which she raised all kinds of vegetables that she harvested in the fall of the year, and then she would can the vegetables to be eaten during the winter. We had what is known as a springhouse, which is a stone structure built in the middle of a small mountain creek, completely enclosed, used to keep homemade butter and other food cool and keep them from spoiling. I can remember sitting on the front porch of their farmhouse pumping the wooden handle of the butter churn up and down to separate the milk fat from the milk. The milk fat was actually used to make the butter.

The owner of the farm my aunt and uncle sharecropped on had a son who everyone called RL. We were friends and often hunted and fished together. We also liked to target practice with our .22 caliber rifles. We would take one of the old wooden matches and stick it head up in a crack in a fence post then walk off twenty-five yards and start shooting at the match head, trying to actually strike the match head, causing it to fire up, without knocking down or disturbing the wooden part of the match. We became such good shots that we could light the match nine out of ten times.

One snowy Christmas eve, in 1940, my mother came to Woodrow, Kentucky, with the man she had married, Elijah William Gunn. He was a wonderful person who continued to teach me the skills I would need to survive in the not-too-friendly world of post–World War II.

My mother and new stepfather took me back to Louisville to live with them. I will never forget the first place we lived in Louisville, which was in Highland Park. It was a very rough place to grow up in. Almost every day, either in school or on the walk home, I managed to get into a fight, which would later make me afraid of nothing, even combat in war.

One day, when we were living on Crittenden Drive, this kid hit my mother in the back with a brick, and I, being only seven years old, became enraged, so I went to our kitchen, grabbed a big butcher knife, and chased the kid with the intent of killing him. Thank God someone stopped me before I did kill him.

My stepbrother Bill and I were out riding our bicycles one day when Bill lost control and rode into a ditch where his bare foot hit a broken whiskey bottle, cutting his foot severely. I finally got him home and got medical help for him.

The only real dad I ever had was my mother's second husband, Elijah William Gunn, who was an Irishman. He lost his first wife in an automobile accident and injured his son, Elijah William Gunn, Jr., also known as Bill, causing him to be handicapped with a right arm all but useless.

My stepdad had a laundry route, working for the Beha Laundry Company, also referred to as Ma-Beha, in the eastern part of Louisville, Kentucky. I worked part time for him after school and Saturdays until I started high school. He would tell me stories about when he was a young man, such as when he was in the CCC work program during the Depression, and when he went to Chicago for work, where he watched the famous

Jack Dempsey box at Soldier Field. He was the heavyweight champion at the time. My stepdad was a good man, with only a few faults, that being a bad Irish temper and a gambling habit, which my mother helped him with by paying off his gambling debts.

My mother and stepdad argued a lot, mostly about money or the lack of it and about the discipline of me and my stepbrother Bill. Mom and Dad finally agreed that Mom would discipline me and Dad his son Bill.

We moved a lot during those early years, and I am not sure if the reason for the frequent moving was the lack of money or my mother's depression and compulsion with moving.

One day, when we were living on Preston Street, Bill and I went to the corner grocery store, and as I was walking up the steps, a black kid, who was about sixteen years old, spit on me. I felt like an erupting volcano as I punched his face at least thirty or forty times. The only thing that saved his live was that his mother pulled me off him. I was twelve years old at the time.

I finally got through the ninth grade at Halleck Hall, which is now Manual High School. I was in the limbo age—immature, shy, and a loner. I tried music, attempted to learn to play the clarinet and saxophone, but mostly I was only successful in splitting reeds on the instrument mouthpieces and making the most horrible screeching sound the music teacher said he had ever heard.

I started high school at dear old Louisville Male High School located at Brook and Breckenridge streets. There was a four-story brick house across the street from Male High School, and on the fourth floor was a woman (prostitute) who laid her large breasts on the windowsill, tempting the high school boys and inviting them up to her place for some sexual action. While attending Male High School, I tried sports and tried out for the football team but was too small and wasn't heavy enough. Then I went out for basketball, but the coach said I played too rough and I was always fouling out. I finally found the sport of wrestling, which I was good at, and stayed with that sport for about two years. I then became interested in boxing and started fighting Golden Gloves at Columbia Gym where Cassius Clay, born on January 17, 1942, trained. He was later known as Muhammad Ali. One night I was boxing a guy who fought in a low crouch, keeping his head down and completely covered up. I became so frustrated by his style that I hit him right on top of his head, knocking him out and breaking a bone in my right hand, which ended my thoughts of being a professional boxer.

I was doing pretty well in every subject except English, which I hated. Finally, the principal called Mom and I into his office to inform us that I was failing English, and I would have to go through the eleventh grade again. That was when I decided to drop out of school and go to work. When I left school, I drifted from job to job.

My mom was receiving some child support for years from my biological dad and had saved up enough money to buy me a car, which was a 1946 Ford Convertible with a white top, shiny black paint, and Cadillac hubcaps. It was a real cool car and got me a lot of friends, as well as many girlfriends. I finally saved enough money to buy my first motorcycle, which was a 1942 spring fork, forty-five-cubic-inch, V-twin Harley. My friends

Doug Black and Jere Houk rode the wheels off those old forty-five-cubic-inch Harleys.

In those days, when I was eighteen, I loved riding my Harley-Davidson motorcycle. One day, when I rode my motorcycle to Jeffersonville, Indiana, I discovered the Jeffersonville Boat and Machine Company, also known as Jeff Boat. After watching some second-class welders welding flat weld on river barge bottoms (hulls), I decided I could weld as good as those guys, so I went and filled out an application. I was given a flat-weld test, and I was hired the same day. I loved welding at Jeff Boat. I finally became proficient enough to take the first-class, all-position welder test, which I passed on the first take. The test consisted of welding butt metal in three positions, which were flat, vertical, and overhead welds. Then the three plates were cut into two pieces and bent double, as well as Magnafluxed, using a red liquid dye first, and then if there was a flaw in the weld, the red dye would be pulled out of the crack in the weld up through the white die and indicate where the hairline crack was at.

After I made first-class all-position welder, I joined the Shipbuilder Workers of America Union and started attending union meetings once a month. I believe this was when I started becoming addicted to alcohol. Practically everyone who worked at Jeff Boat drank, to think the shipyard was such a dangerous place to work at.

We had a big shipfitter who was about six feet, six inches tall and weighed close to three hundred pounds. He was the heavyweight boxing champion of the US Sixth Fleet in the navy during World War II. He was sort of a bully, and a lot of people fought with him during their work shift. One night he was sitting on top of a stern section (rear) of a barge, which was under construction, drinking from a gallon jug of alcohol. I climbed a ladder that was on the back of the stern and struck an electric arc under his butt. I had the welding machine set on reverse polarity and used a 5/16-inch straight polarity rod, which caused a huge blast of electrical energy when the welding rod touched metal. The results were "Big Townsend" jumped off the stern and fell about twenty feet. He never pushed his weight around again.

Another incident worth writing about is one day Morris Welsh, who was a shipfitter working with his helper, was driving a steel wedge into a dog, which was welded to one part of the hull, and when the wedge is driven into the dog, it forces the other sheet of metal up against the other piece of steel, making a lap figuration. Anyway, Morris was hitting the steel wedge with a ten-pound sledgehammer and somehow miscalculated the sledgehammer blow and hit his helper in the forehead. The helper screamed and started running down the crane tracks. We finally caught him and discovered his forehead caved in. We rushed him to the Jeffersonville Hospital, where he was treated for a concussion and kept in for over a week.

At Jeff Boat, there was a shipfitter named Morris, who did not like the new yard supervisor, so he dropped a two-by-twelve board, fifteen feet long, on his supervisor as he walked under the scaffold that was on the side of the bow. He was taken to the hospital and was never again seen at Jeff Boat.

We had a high-tracked crane moving this huge piece of 5/16-inch sheet steel and three ironworkers were riding the load.

Two other ironworkers were at the load destination point when the crane boom just collapsed. It killed our five ironworkers.

From time to time, we would get one of the river paddle wheel boats in for hull repair, and we would have to pull it in on our dry dock, float the dock, and the ship fitters would cut out the rusted hull steel and replace it with new metal. Then the first-class welders would come behind them and weld the inside lap seams and then the outside lap steel, which was all overhead welding. When we were working on the old river paddle wheel boats or the river tow boats, the owners would leave a cook on board, and she would feed us all the good food we could eat.

As I mentioned earlier, I loved riding my motorcycle, which was a Harley-Davidson Chopper with a 1941 spring fork and a seventy-four-cubic-inch engine stroked to an eighty cubic inch with a hot cam, dual carbs, and straight-through exhaust pipes. I usually rode with two of my friends, Tony Neff and Jere Houk. We were out riding one night somewhere behind Iroquois Park in the boondocks, going around a curve, when the front tire of Tony's sixty-one-cubic-inch Harley blew. He lost control, going through an apple orchard without once hitting a tree!

Tony had always been a good friend and a good worker, but when he married his girlfriend Sue, he just quit work and forced Sue to support him and their two kids. I still don't know to this day why he changed so much and became a bum. He didn't drink or use drugs, so it must have been a mental problem.

Jere and I were out another night, and while we were sitting at a stoplight, revving our engines (like all motorcycle riders do), his suicide clutch cable broke, and Jere took off out of control. I shouted to him to bail out, and he just rolled off his Harley backward, and the Harley slid under a big truck. If Jere had been on the bike, he would have been dead that night. When I enlisted in the regular army, I didn't see Jere again until around 1977, when I went home to Louisville to visit my mom. Jere had almost thirty years in at the Louisville Police Department.

Another night Tony and I were riding side by side on our Harley Choppers when this jerk came up behind us and started to hit our rear tires with his bumper. About that time, Tony told me to split, and I went to the right, while he went to the left. The jerk went through and ahead of us. Tony pulled out a .38 pistol and put six slugs through his rear window. Needless to say, the driver of the car put his foot in the carb, and we never saw him again.

Then there was the time a bunch of us were out drinking and riding, and getting almost wasted, we left a bar. One of our riders was so wasted he kept falling off his Harley, so we put him back on his Chopper and gave him a push. He rode pretty good until he had to stop for a red light, and then he would fall off again, but we finally got him home in one piece.

I had just broken in my rebuilt, hopped-up Chopper, and I wanted to see how fast it would go. I had a 160-miles-per-hour speedometer and, riding the gas tank without a shield, pegged the speedometer at 160 miles per hour, but I had to back off the throttle when a speed wobble occurred (vibration of frame), which could have shaken my Harley to pieces if I had stayed on the throttle.

Love

It was about this time, when I was eighteen years old, that Jere and I were out riding in my hopped-up 1946 Ford Convertible and decided to stop for a milkshake at Taylor's Drug Store at the corner of Preston Street and Eastern Parkway, right across St. Joseph's Hospital and cattycorner from my favorite hamburger place, White Castle. We were sitting there when we became acquainted with two girls who we later married. The girl I met was Carolyn Schwencker, who I dated for almost a year. Jere began dating my girlfriend's friend and eventually married her. I think they had two children, and their marriage ended in a divorce.

We decided to get married because she kept telling me that she had to get away from her family and also because of great sex. *Big mistake!*

Carolyn and I married in July of 1954. I had enlisted in the Seventh Special Infantry Company USMCR in February of 1954 as soon as I turned nineteen years old. The Seventh Special Infantry Company was oriented toward special operations designed along the lines of the Second World War Marine Raiders (Commandos). The Seventh Special was trained in jungle warfare, cold-weather mountain warfare, and underwater demolition (UDT). Our outfit was used as commando aggressors operating behind enemy lines, sabotaging enemy communications, water supplies, and as six-men ambush teams, also as sniper teams, which while operating behind enemy lines, assassinated high-ranking enemy officers and reconned information back to marine commanders on troop movements, as well as enemy arms being used. We had some scary incidents during our training, such as, while going through the marine infiltration course at Camp Lejeune in Jacksonville, North Carolina, I was behind one marine who was having some problems. We were in pouring down rain, mud, TNT exploding all around us, and .30-caliber Browning machine guns firing live ammunition thirty-six inches above the ground. Anyway, the marine in front of me came to this log, which he had to go over. Keeping as low as possible because of the live machine-gun fire, he slid his M-1 Garand rifle over the log and started to slide his body over the log when he abruptly started to rise into the path of the live ammo bullets passing over his head. I, almost without thinking about it, grabbed his battle fatigue collar and forced him straight down into the muddy infiltration course and, at the same time, screaming, "CEASE-FIRE!" After the live fire ceased, I pulled the marine's face out of the mud and asked him why he started to stand up in the line of the live fire bullets. He said there was a rattlesnake on the other side of the log.

The commander of the Seventh Special Infantry Company thought I should be recognized for saving the marine's life, so he gave me a "meritorious promotion" to permanent corporal. My best friend, James E. Mulloy, who was right behind me when the incident on the infiltration course happened, told our commander all about it. I hadn't seen Jim Mulloy or talked to him for over fifty years when I was browsing the marine corps websites and happened to locate him and his phone number in Oceanside, California. I called Jim, and we communicated for about six months until President Bush started the Iraq war, and we haven't talked since. It is too bad that Jim had what I call blind patriotism and believed any war was justified as long as an American president said so.

During the same training period, we were to fire at silhouette targets, and in 1954, we did not have automated pop-up targets, so we dug five feet deep, about thirty inches in diameter, one-man spider holes, where a marine would raise the target by hand while we fired at the target. One marine got heatstroke and could not stand the rifle bullets hitting so close to him, so he jumped out of his hole and started running parallel to the firing line while live bullets were being fired all along the line. He was not hit only by the grace of God.

Another time, we were firing at bull's-eye targets on Able (250 yards) and Baker (500 yards) courses, where we had marines that were not on the firing line, raising and lowering targets, spotting bullet hits, then raising targets to firing position again. There was a red line with a warning sign, "DO NOT CROSS RED LINE WHILE LIVE FIRE IS IN PROGRESS." However, one marine, for some reason, left his target and crossed the red danger line. He was by a .30-caliber armor, the bullet piercing through his neck, then down, hitting his heart and killing him instantly.

We had so many close calls that it was just like real combat in Vietnam. One day, while training at Camp Lejeune, this marine instructor was demonstrating the proper use and purpose of a marine MK-1 fragmentation grenade. The grenade must have had a defective fuse because as soon as he pulled the pin and released the lever, the grenade exploded in his hand, killing him instantly.

During this same training period, we were practicing bayonet drills, which consisted of parry left or right (forcing the enemy's weapon to the left or right with your rifle with attached bayonet) and upper-butt stroke, where you hit the enemy under the chin with the butt of your rifle after the parry maneuver; then the bayonet slash, where after the butt stroke and as you are bringing your weapon with bayonet down, you slash the enemy's throat, then thrust the bayonet straight into the enemy's chest. Sometimes, on the thrust movement, the bayonet would stick between bones or cartilage, making it almost impossible to remove the bayonet from the enemy's chest. In the case of a stuck bayonet, you have to fire a round from the rifle that recoils backward when fired, freeing the bayonet.

During the 1950s, when I was in the Seventh Special Infantry Company (Special Ops) USMCR, we had an unusual/unofficial, unauthorized element of training known by marines as the blood pit. The pit was a trench dug in the sand, three feet deep, ten feet wide, and fifteen feet long. The object of the exercise was to line ten to twelve Marines up on each side of the pit, then blow a whistle, which signaled all the marines to jump into the blood pit and start fighting with any type fighting authorized. The last marine standing received medical attention and then was granted three-day liberty (leave). This was rough training and not officially authorized by the marine corps, but the pit was the best way to train us for hand-to-hand combat with the enemy.

MARRIAGE

My wife Carolyn and I were doing okay with our marriage until we moved to 1004 East Oak Street, about a half block from her mother's. That's when her personality started to change. She also wanted to try to have a baby. She got pregnant, and James Robert Detheridge, Jr., was born in July of 1957. He was a good baby almost all the time. The next year Carolyn had a little girl who was named Belinda. From the very start, she was awful, as she cried all the time, day and night. I was working the 4:00 p.m. to 12:00 a.m. shift at Tube Turns, where Carolyn's dad got me a pipe-welding job. This job paid more money, but I hated the work. I could not sleep because of Belinda's constant crying. I began to stop and have a few beers after work. The more stress I had at home because of Belinda crying and arguments with Carolyn and her parents, the more I drank until I became a borderline alcoholic. One night a shift boss, who knew nothing about welding, was constantly on my back about the quality of the welds. He made me so mad that I hit him, knocking him about twenty-feet over steel pipes. The next day, they said I was laid off. I tried other jobs but could not keep a steady job because of the stress at home and my increased drinking. In 1960, Carolyn finally separated from me.

Since I was not working, I drifted for two years before I enlisted in the army. Carolyn had me incarcerated for lack of child support. Then she and a jerk named Sam Bennett said that if I would let him adopt Jimmy and Belinda, I would be left alone, so I signed the papers and joined the army. Sam Bennett adopted Jimmy and Belinda, changing their last names to Bennett. The last time I saw my children, Jimmy and Belinda, was in 1962, prior to enlisting in the regular army.

When I left Louisville, I went through basic training at Fort Knox, near Elizabethtown, Kentucky. About three-quarters of the way through our training, we were on a twenty-mile forced night march, humping a ninety-pound pack, a five-pound steel helmet, two canteens of water, and a ten-pound rifle, which amounted to over a hundred pounds. While we were going through a valley, back in the boondocks behind Fort Knox, we were hit with large amounts of tear gas (CS), so we put on our gas masks, cleared them, and proceeded to advance in a military skirmish line.

On my left flank, I noticed a trooper who was having trouble clearing the gas from his gas mask. He proceeded to throw away all his equipment and started running. I knew there was a three-hundred-foot cliff directly in the direction he was headed, so I ran after him and managed to tackle him right before he went over the cliff. We both found ourselves entangled in wild blackberry bushes. I completed the twenty-mile forced march with some difficulty because of pain in my right leg. When the march was over, I went to the Fort Knox Hospital for treatment and was diagnosed with tendonitis of the Achilles tendon in my right leg. Toward the end of my basic training, a woman, Wilma, who I had been seeing, started picking me up at ten o'clock each night, and we would drive to Iroquois Park. We would just sit and talk until two or three o'clock in the morning. This relationship with Wilma was just a case of both of us needing someone, and we were there for each other at this crucial time in our lives.

Upon completion of basic training, I was assigned to the Forty-Fifth Artillery Brigade and stationed at Arlington Heights, Illinois. We were the Chicago-Gary Air Defense because of our Nike Hercules Missiles. I pulled guard duty around our concrete, steel reinforced war rec-room with ten-foot thick walls and ceilings. We had a very complex, highly sophisticated early warning system radar, which was part of the Chicago-Gary Air Defense System. One night we were tracking B-58 Hustler Bombers flying out of Oklahoma, testing our defenses, when the radar operator picked up a "blip" on his scope, which was not an air force B-58 bomber. He asked for and received permission to scramble fighters out of Truax Field in Madison, Wisconsin. The fighter took off and picked up the UFOs on their radar. When they approached the UFO, it accelerated to what they thought was eighteen thousand miles per hour, straight up, losing contact with our fighter planes. Also, when I was with the Forty-Fifth Brigade (known as the Fighting Forty-Fifth), when two of our troopers went to South Side, Chicago, they were severely beaten. When we heard about it, we saddled up 250 airborne troops and cleaned up South Side, Chicago.

The Chicago Police knew we were going to rumble with the South Side hoodlums, and they did not even try to stop us.

I was with another Kentuckian in his 1955 Oldsmobile, when we drove up to a human chain across the street. I told my friend to take them out, so he pulled his gear selector down into super low and floor-boarded the gas pedal. When his car hit the human chain, bodies flew everywhere. We took most of them out in hand-to-hand fighting, using chains, brass knuckles, and two-by-four wooden clubs.

And War Army Incidents

After I enlisted in the regular army (RA) and went to Fort Knox for basic training, we were separated into platoons and squads. One day a black soldier from Chicago, who was about six feet tall and weighed in at two hundred fifty pounds, was playing the drums on the rear steps of our World War II wooden barracks when another troop from Chicago, an Italian by the name of Frank Caliendo, got tired of the noise and proceeded to pour a bucket of water on the would-be drummer. This black trooper got mad and chased Frank into the latrine (bathroom), where he grabbed a wooden towel rod, two inches in diameter and six feet long, with the intent of beating Frank to death. He swung twice and missed then said to Frank, "I am going to kill you," so I stepped between him and Frank. He paused, thinking about it, laid down the wood towel rod, and left the latrine. When basic training was over, Frank and I got orders for the Forty-Fifth Artillery Brigade in Arlington Heights, Illinois, northwest of Chicago. Frank took me to his home in Chicago for dinner and introduced me to his family as "the trooper who saved his life" in basic training.

One day, about halfway through basic training, we were alerted for a twenty-mile forced march, which we started on the next day. It was getting dark, and we were still marching along the side of a gravel road when we heard a rumbling sound. I knew that it was tanks in the marine corps, so I screamed, "Hit the ditch!" And sure enough, a column of tanks came racing by without running lights, and if we had not hit the ditch, we would have been run over.

All infantry units be, it the army or marine corps, have infiltration courses and obstacle courses. While at Fort Knox in basic training, our company has to go through the infiltration course at night. Since I had been through all this training, the field first sergeant told me to go through the infiltration course with each group going through. There were five groups. I carried an army flashlight with red lens to flash in case one of our troopers got scared and froze up, in which case I had to kick him in the butt and get him moving again. In case I couldn't get the troop to move because of the live .30-caliber machine-gun fire, I flash the red light, and the gun ceased fire. I went through the infiltration course five times that night, and by the end of the night, I had worn holes in my battle fatigue elbows and knees, with blood seeping out. I was the last trooper to complete that infiltration course that night.

One day an E-7 sergeant came over to me, and when I talked to him, he asked me if my dad was Charley Detheridge. I told him yes, and he said that he and my dad were in the Army Horse Calvary together, and my dad, being his sergeant, always had him cleaning horse crap out of the horse stables.

While still in basic training, we were being taught hand-to-hand combat by this sergeant, and when I came up against him, I used marine judo and jujitsu to throw him. I threw his rear end. He asked me if I had prior hand-to-hand combat training. I told him yes, marine corps judo and jujitsu, plus marine hand-to-hand and street fighting.

One night, still in basic, we set up camp in a night defensive position on the side of this steep hill, putting two shelter halves together, making a pup tent. Two troopers set up their tent across a natural drainage of rain area, and I told my friend Frank they were in trouble if it rained that night. About midnight, we got a gully washer of a rain, and I heard these two troops screaming their tent, sleeping bags, and packs had been washed away.

One night, while in the army at Forty-Fifth Brigade, I decided to go to the NCO club for some relaxation. I ordered a beer at the bar and was just sitting there relaxing when this black NCO (noncommissioned officer) sat on the barstool next to me. After a few minutes, he said to me, "You're prejudiced against blacks, aren't you?" I don't know why, but I completely lost control, hit him as hard as I could, and walked out.

About once a week, the troops in our barracks would have what is known as a bare-knuckle fight. The rules were that the first fighter knocked down lost. The troops would bet money almost like a real professional fight. We would post lookouts to let us know if the military police (MPs) were coming.

One year, while in the army, I went home to Louisville to see my mom and sister. I went down to a local bar wearing my winter dress green uniform, and while sitting at the bar,

I was suddenly turned around and hit with a sucker punch, which knocked me up onto the bar. I came off the bar and went after the jerk. He swung again and missed, so I picked up a metal barstool and hit him square in the face. Blood went everywhere, and he went down. I heard a police siren and ran out the back door.

While in the army, I worked with military classified documents and made daily courier runs to Fort Sheridan, which was located in Highland Park, Illinois. I was what is known as a courier under arms because I carried a fully loaded 1911 .45 caliber semiautomatic A-1 pistol. One day, on my way to Fort Sheridan, this big black limo started to pass my truck, and this guy who looked Italian stared at me. I drove on, and I could see the limo parked alongside the road. When I passed, the limo took off, and before he could get alongside of me, I pulled my .45 pistol and laid my right hand on the door, pointed right at the limo, when it pulled up beside me. When they saw the pistol, they took off for good. I wrote down the license plate number and had the military police run the number. They found out the limo was a mobster's car.

I only have one other comment about the army, and that is the army is the most disorganized, poorly trained branch of service I have ever been associated with; the marine corps is the best trained, most professional fighting force in the world.

I had been with the Forty-Fifth Brigade for over a year when I met a woman named Sally at Crystal Lake, Illinois. We just clicked from the start, and we were married on December 30, 1963. My three-year tour with the army was coming to a close in August of 1965, so I decided to separate rather than reenlist. I found work as a welder and worked several jobs. Then I applied for a job as an apprentice electrician with Bruning Manufacturing Company. I was working twelve hours a day, six days a week. It didn't take me long to tire of civilian life, so I enlisted in the air force at the Chicago Air Force Recruiting Office. I retained my army rank and was given my base of choice, which was Ninth Weather Wing, stationed at McClellan Air Force Base in Sacramento, California. My wife stayed in Chicago long enough to sell our mobile home and came to California to join me in April of 1966. I received orders for duty in Vietnam with a departure date of September 12, 1966. I packed my duffel bag, and Sally drove me to Travis Air Force Base for my MAC flight to Saigon, Vietnam. We landed at Tan Son Nhut Air Force Base at 1100 hours on September 13, 1966. I was told to spend the night at the transit barracks on perimeter of the air force base. At 2200 hours, the Vietcong sapper units hit the air base at the same location of the transit barracks, where there were fifty unarmed military men in transit. The Vietcong fought their way through the perimeter defense, forcing the air force security police to retreat (run), leaving forty-nine unarmed military, including myself, to deal with the Vietcong. I told everyone that the only chance we had was to block all entrances to the transit barracks, which would force the Vietcong to enter the one entrance to the transit barracks single file.

The day I landed at Tan Son Nhut AFB on September 13, 1966, was memorable in that there were fifty unarmed troops in this Quonset hut when the Vietcong attacked our hut, and when they came in the door, we engaged them in hand-to-hand combat. The Vietcong came through the door firing his AK-47 rifle on rock and roll, hitting this troop next to me in the head causing his head to explode, throwing blood, brain tissue, and bone fragments all over me; and to this day, this man's blood is still on me and I can't wash it off. This actually happened to me. We had two KIA (dead) and fifteen WIA (wounded in action).

Our plan worked great, and we jumped them in hand-to-hand combat. We managed to take some AK-47 Russian rifles away from them, which enabled us to finally force them to pull back, carrying their dead and wounded with them.

The next day I received orders detaching me from the air force and reattaching me to the 134th Aviation Company (C7-A Caribou) United States Army in Can Tho, Vietnam (IV Corps), which was in the Mekong Delta along the Bassac River of extreme South Vietnam. When I reported to the army orderly room, the army first sergeant told me that I was no longer in the air force but in the army and would pull the same duties as other army troops, which included guard duty, air base security, air base jungle reconnaissance to keep the Vietcong away from the air base. After I was in the delta for about a month, I met some army special forces troops who were with Company D Fifth Special Forces. After talking to them for a while and telling them of my marine corps and army training, I was asked if I would like to go on some night ambushes with them. Needless to say, I jumped at the chance; so for the next three months, the Fifth Special Forces and I hunted the Vietcong at night, and I performed my regular army duties during the day. I didn't get much sleep. I don't have an accurate KIA body count of the

Vietcong killed because they carried their wounded and dead from the ambush site.

One night I volunteered for a night ambush mission with Fifth Special Forces and Vietnamese Rangers. We started our long march back to base before daylight, marching route step, when a ranger stepped on an antipersonnel mine in front of me, and luckily, our intervals were about thirty feet apart. He was killed, and some of us were pretty shook up. When we were within a click, we started to cross a creek, and I noticed a mud-covered rock. I picked it up and put it in my jungle fatigue pants pocket. I carried that rock during the rest of my Vietnam tour and even took it back to the world with me, where it lay in a drawer for twenty years. One day I found it, and since I was taking a jewelry-making class at a local Cheyenne Community College, I decided it would be cool to make a ring out of the stone, which was a tiger eye. With the ring made, I decided to give it to my sister, Carolyn, one year when she visited me in Cheyenne, Wyoming, at Christmastime. Years later, my sister wrote to tell me she had discovered that a tiger eye stone represents protection, and she felt God had allowed me to find it as a sign that he would protect me throughout the war. I told her I believed the same thing. Essentially, what we did was hunt the Vietcong like I did growing up in the country and hills of Kentucky when hunting raccoons.

One night I came into our command and control area, changed clothes, stuck a .45 caliber pistol in my belt under my shirt, and started out to Mekong Restaurant. Before I could leave, a fourteen-year-old Vietnamese boysan said, “Bob, you no go. You no go.” I started out anyway. Bach, the boysan, couldn’t say "Bob," so he called me "Boob." Then the boysan dropped down to his knees, threw his arms around my legs, and crying said again, "Bob, you no go." That was when I realized he knew something bad was going to happen, so I just stayed where I was.

In about fifteen minutes, we heard a loud explosion and found out that a Vietcong sapper team had thrown an explosive satchel charge into the Mekong Restaurant, killing and wounding a lot of our military. The next day Bach brought me some bananas and other fruits that he had gathered from the jungle. I told Bach that he was a Vietcong, and he said, smiling, "No, no, me just dumb Vietnamese." I laughed and said, "Right." This young boysan saved my life and would do so many times in the future by letting me and the Special Forces know of the future activities of the Vietcong. One day, while pulling daytime guard duty, an old papasan rode his bike up to my guard post, parked it, and then he started walking away. I looked at the papasan, then at the bicycle, and decided something was wrong. I shouted to the papasan, "Lau dae! Mau, mau." (Come here! Hurry, hurry!) He came back to my guard post, and I called over the Vietnamese Police, who discovered the bicycle had plastic explosives wired to a ten-minute timing device. The Vietnamese Police took the old papasan out into the city square (park) and shot him in the head and hauled the body off.

I volunteered to ride shotgun on a six-ton truck going to Binh Thuy Air Force Base, which would be an easy mission, except it was 1930 hours (7:30 p.m.) and the road to Bien Thuy was off-limits after 1830 hours (6:30 p.m.) because of frequent Vietcong ambushes and the planting of land mines.

We had traveled about half of the five miles to Bien Thuy when I heard the sound of a heavy machine gun and could feel the impact of the heavy bullets hitting the back of the truck. The Vietcong gunner was walking the bullets up toward us in the cab of the six-ton truck, so I slid halfway out of my passenger door and returned fire with my M-3 .45-caliber submachine gun. Either I hit the Vietcong gunner or we outran his gun. I will never know for sure what kept Army SP4 and me from being killed.

On another occasion, SP4 got about halfway drunk and decided to steal a Vietnamese boat docked along the Bassac River and go out to what was known as VC Island to see if he could kill some Vietcong. The next morning, he came back wearing two sets of freshly cut Vietcong ears around his neck as trophies. This same soldier got rip-roaring drunk one night and walked into the local nightclub, opened up on rock and roll (full automatic fire) with his captured AK-47 Russian rifle, killing at least twenty people. The unwounded military in the club jumped him and disarmed him. The next day he was shipped to Saigon for a psychiatric evaluation, where he was found to be "certified nuts." He was sent back to the States for treatment/imprisonment.

One day, toward the end of November, I was pulling guard duty and watching this boysan who was shining the shoes of a bunch of military on the other side of the city square, when, all of a sudden, another boysan ran by, grabbed the shoeshine boysan's hat, and they both ran away. A few minutes later, a bomb that was in the shoeshine box exploded, killing twenty-three Americans. It was as if the whole world blew up, and there were body parts and blood flying in every direction, even as far as my guard post about half a block away. That same day, only later, a Buddhist monk sat down in front of my guard post, doused himself with gasoline, struck a match, and set himself on fire. I couldn't leave my guard post, so I was forced to watch and smell him burn to death. The Vietcong invented the suicide bomber weapon. They would recruit children, train them to kill Americans, then fit them with a boom vest hidden under their pajama. They would then approach American troops who would tell them to "Di di. Mau, mau" (Go away. Hurry, hurry"), and if they continued toward us, we would kill them. Almost 100 percent of the time, they had bomb vests on their bodies.

The city of Can Tho was so dangerous that the military could come to Can Tho only from 1200 to 1600 hours (from 12:00 p.m. to 4:00 p.m.).

I went out on night ambush missions with the Special Operations Troops (SEALs and Special Forces) along the Bassac River. The Navy River Patrol boats (PBRs) would drop us off at a predesignated drop area in the vicinity of known Vietcong camps and then come back to pick us up the next morning, if we had survived the night. Quite often, while traveling to the boat drop-off area, the boat would be ambushed along the many meandering twists and bends of the river. At times our PBR would go into a bend in the river and the Vietcong would open up on us with heavy machine guns, mortars, and AK-47 rifles, which was very difficult to survive because of the complete surprise of the river ambush. We always had wounded Americans and heavy damage to our PBR boat. We had a main PBR base aboard a landing craft tank (LST) anchored in the middle of the

Mekong River right at the point where the Bassac River enters the Mekong River. On several occasions, the Vietcong frogmen infiltrated our river defenses at night, planting plastic explosives on our LST and causing some major damage.

When we were on night ambush patrol en route to our selected ambush site, we had to be on the alert for booby traps, which consisted of Punji sticks, sharpened bamboo stakes dipped in human feces driven into a hole and camouflaged with surrounding vegetation. We also encountered dud 250- and 500-pound bombs dropped by our fast mover planes, which were either command-detonated or trip-wire-detonated. There were also spring-loaded platform devices, which had stakes and were activated by trip wire. These devices would hit a trooper from the side, penetrating his body, killing him instantly, pining him to a tree on the opposite side of the trail.

One night, while with the Special Forces on a night ambush, we fired up what we thought was a small force of VC, but it turned out to be around three hundred Vietcong. We had to call in Puff the Magic Dragon, which was an old World War II C-47 airplane fitted with 20mm Gatling Guns. While Puff was firing up the Vietcong, we (myself and some Special Forces Troops) evacuated the area quickly. If we did not have Puff to bail us out, we would have been overran and probably all of us killed.

We had armed forces radio, and in November of 1966, *Hanoi Hanna* broadcast to the American troops in the Mekong Delta that the "Glorious North Vietnamese Army (NVA) and the Delta Vietcong would attack and overrun Can Tho Air Base and Bien Thuy Air Force Base on Christmas Eve. The enemy attacked just as *Hanoi Hanna* had aired on December 24, and the battle lasted from December 24 through December 26. We had some sapper units that slipped through the wire and managed to kill some of our troops before we could kill them. An especially sad KIA was a seventeen-year-old army troop who had his throat cut from ear to ear. Either he was not alert during the attack or he went to sleep on his post.

We had some killed in action and many wounded. The enemy suffered very heavy casualties but, as usual, carried most of their dead and wounded with them when they broke contact with our forces. During the attack in Bien Thuy Air Force Base, American casualties were light, but some of the K-9 dog handlers and their dogs were shot up pretty bad.

After the big battle, we had to police up our dead and wounded and also repair the damage to our air base, planes, and the city of Can Tho.

We had Navy Patrol Boats River (PBR) stationed just upstream from Can Tho. These boats were responsible for stopping the Vietcong from running guns down through Cambodia, up the Bassac River, and on to the Iron Triangle northwest of Saigon. This operation was known as the Can Tho corridor, and it was hard to catch the Vietcong boats because they moved at night and laid up in coves or tributaries. I went on these PBRs several times, and we sunk a lot of Vietnamese boats, as well as stopping the movement of arms and ammunition.

On some of the PBRs, we had marine snipers who would set up night ambushes along the Bassac River. The way the snipers would operate is that they would have a couple of Navy SEALs infiltrate to a designated place in the jungle, sit down and start talking and making enough noise so that the Vietcong could hear and locate them, and then just as the Vietcong were taking aim at the SEALs, the marine sniper would take them out one by one. Years later, in the year 2000, I was at the VA Hospital in Denver, Colorado, and heard someone call my name. When I looked around, I saw one of the marine snipers I served with in the Mekong Delta. He was in a wheelchair. He had taken a 7.39mm slug from an AK-47 in the lower spine and was now a paraplegic. I told him I was sorry it was him who was hit.

The Fifth Special Forces were also responsible for training the Vietnamese Special Forces, and when they went out on night ambush and recon missions, I tagged along, hoping to see some action. One night, while accompanying the Vietnamese Special Forces, I was walking in the slack position, which is right behind the point man, when we were ordered to halt. While waiting for the squad to resume moving, I stepped off the trail a few yards. The jungle was so thick I decided to part some of the jungle because I thought I had heard something that was not a jungle sound. When I parted the leaves and branches, I stood there face-to-face with an armed Vietcong trail watcher. Before I could get a shot off, he had simply disappeared. If I had not found this trail watcher, he would have shot our rear guard or set up an ambush further down the high-speed trail.

Bronze Star Medal with V Device

Because of my volunteering for dangerous missions with the regular army, Fifth Special Forces and Navy Seals, the three commanders of their respected Special Operations Units, approached my air force commander, requesting that I be nominated for the Bronze Star with V Device for valor during combat operations. I was not aware of this medal nomination until we moved north and my commander asked me to write my own citation for the Bronze Star with V Device. I told him I didn't think it was right for me to write my own citation, so the air force, which didn't care one way or the other, just dropped the citation idea, and I didn't get the medal. Years later, I wished that I had written the citation and gotten the Bronze Star medal because it would have been easier to prove to VA Benefits that I had been in some very serious combat situations.

On January 1, 1967, the air force personnel attached and trained by the Army 134th Aviation Company C7-A Caribou aircraft technicians accepted operational control of the C7-A Caribou cargo aircraft, and we moved north to the II Corps, which was very close to the Seventeenth Parallel and North

Vietnam. Some of our planes were stationed at Phu Cat, Cam Ranh Bay, and other remote military sites. After we moved north, our aircraft and personnel were defended by marines or one of the two airborne units, which were the Eighty-Second Airborne out of Fort Bragg, North Carolina, or the 101st Airborne stationed out of Fort Campbell, at Hopkinsville, Kentucky.

After we moved north and got organized, I volunteered to help the aircraft crews when they flew in ammunition and supplies to Special Forces A Teams, who manned remote fire bases in some of the most dangerous areas of South Vietnam. On more than one occasion, we flew into these firebases when they were under attack by the North Vietnamese Army (NVA) and had our planes shot up pretty badly. Another mission we had was to pick up dead American and Vietnamese who were in body bags and to bring these dead back to Tan Sun Nhut Air Force Base in Saigon for the flight back to McGuire Air Force Base for burial processing. On one of these body bag flights, we were hit by NVA .51-caliber radar-controlled machine guns, knocking out our starboard engine, forcing us to climb out of the range of the Vietcong. .51-caliber radar-armed guns. But then we had another problem. Because we climbed so high, the day's old dead military in the black body bags started to explode. The body bags burst open, and pieces of dead soldiers and marines flew all over the interior of our aircraft. Most of us on board upchucked. After we returned to our airfield, we had already dropped off what was remaining of the dead and the body bags, but then, after landing, we had the gruesome job of trying to clean up the human remains that were still in the aircraft. We never did get it completely clean, and the odor remained no matter what we tried.

During the big American military buildup of 1966 in Vietnam, the North Vietnamese were sending infantry and political cadre into South Vietnam to recruit Vietcong from the cities and hamlets. These cadres would visit the rural hamlets at night, forcibly taking the farmer's rice and young men ages twelve years old and up. If a hamlet chief refused to cooperate with the NVA and Vietcong, they would first murder the hamlet chief, and if there was still resistance, the NVA and Vietcong would start killing the women and children. The job of NVA political officers was to convince the hamlet Vietnamese that the communist way of life and their type of government was superior to the American democracy. They did this by printing lies in pamphlets, through anti-American lectures, and when they felt safe, would show films of the Vietcong and national Vietnamese armies in combat, always when they were winning a battle.

As I said, the Vietcong and NVA were having their big buildup in 1966, and it took their military two years to become strong enough to launch their big Tet military offensive of 1968, when the Vietcong and National Vietnamese Armies simultaneously attacked 120 South Vietnamese cities. The Americans and south were caught off balance and surprised but quickly regrouped and turned defeat into victories all over South Vietnam. The Vietcong were virtually wiped out and did not ever have an effective fighting force for the remainder of the war.

Tet is a Vietnam national holiday, being to the Vietnamese Christmas, New Year's, and several other holidays celebrated in this one Tet holiday. Every year of the war, the North and South Vietnamese declared a truce to celebrate Tet, and fighting stopped during this truce. The Vietcong and NVA took advantage of this truce by deploying more troops from North Vietnam and building up their supply and ammunitions, carrying them down the Ho Chi Min Trail, which was actually a high-speed trail of hard-packed earth and gravel, concealed almost entirely by triple-canopy jungle growth. Triple-canopy jungle is when the jungle trees grow so thick and so tall (one hundred feet in height) that the jungle completely hides enemy movement and the trails the enemy used.

The only way we found out about these high-speed trails was to send out light recon teams, who would locate these trails, call in artillery coordinates, which made them unusable for a day or two.

We were fighting an unwinnable war because of the blunders of our government and the fact that we were using mostly "conventional warfare tactics." Also, when we went into contact with the enemy, we were told to go for a high body count and then withdraw after the battles, enabling the enemy force to reoccupy the land we had driven them from. In other words, we were trying to win the war through attrition (killing so many of the Vietcong and NVA) that they would quit fighting. It was a stupid idea because the Vietcong and NVA had around 850,000 troops in the field fighting the American, South Vietnamese, Koreans, and Australians, who had a total combat strength of not more than ninety thousand frontline troops. The only way we could have won this war was to eliminate congressional control and, when land was occupied, during and after a battle, to hold that land by permanently occupying that land with allied troops and constantly fighting, occupying land, and moving north, leaving none of the Vietcong and NVA alive until we pushed the enemy all the way back to Hanoi and completely occupying the entire country and killing every Vietcong and NVA that was fighting against us. But as it turned out, the American press convinced the American people that the Americans and South Vietnamese were defeated in the Great NVA and Vietcong Offensive of 1968, when we actually won these battles and the Vietcong was almost annihilated, never to be an effective force again.

Air Superiority/ Artillery

It is my personal opinion that if our ground forces (grunts) had not been able to call in AI-E Skyraiders and JETS Fighter Bombers plus Puff the Magic Dragon (a C-47 WWII cargo plane equipped with .20 millimeter guns and heavy artillery) when they were in danger of being overrun by the hordes of superbly trained North Vietnamese Army (NVA), the war would have been lost by the United States Armed Forces much earlier than the ten years the NVA fought us, reason being the marines and the army infantry fought in Vietnam for thirteen months (marines) and twelve months (army), which resulted in experienced jungle fighters being rotated back to the world after their one-year combat tour and being replaced by inexperienced boots who were lucky if they survived three months without being WIA'd or KIA'd.

Because of the American press, the cold feet of our government, and the fact that the South Vietnamese would not fight for their own country and freedom, we started withdrawing American troops after the Tet offensive and were completely out of Vietnam by 1975. We told the South Vietnamese they could win without American help against North Vietnam, but as it turned out, we withdrew all our ground forces, aircraft, armor, and left the South Vietnamese army nothing to fight the communists hoards with, nothing to defend themselves with except small arms (rifles and pistols).

When I went to Vietnam in 1966, I was a healthy 160-pound man, and when I returned in 1967, I was sick with chronic sinusitis, chronic bronchitis, was spitting up hunks of clotted blood, and had lost weight, down to 130 pounds, not to mention having jungle rot on my feet (layers of skin peels off until there is just meat and blood). I returned back to the world with an assignment to Vandenberg Air Force Base in Lompoc, California. I was given a physical examination and was told that I had fungus growing in my ears, nostrils, and sinus cavities, also jungle rot on different parts of my body was confirmed.

I took a thirty-day leave to pick up my wife and son James in Chicago then went to Louisville, Kentucky, to visit my family and drove back to California.

I stayed at Vandenberg for three years before I got restless and volunteered for duty in Alaska. I was sent to the air force noncommissioned officer academy for six weeks in Albuquerque, New Mexico. When I returned to Vandenberg, I had orders for Alaska. My wife and I bought a new 1970 three-quarter-ton Dodge truck and also bought a truck camper for our trip to Alaska.

After I finished processing out of Vandenberg Air Force Base, we stocked up the camper with food and water and also filled both of the truck gas tanks; each tank held thirty gallons. We started up through Northern California and made our first overnight at Rough River, Oregon. The next stop was Bellingham, Washington. We made several stops in British Columbia, Canada, and we finally came to Whitehorse, British Columbia, where the blacktop ended and the gravel road started and continued for 1,205 miles through some of the roughest wilderness I have ever seen outside of Vietnam. The gas stations were 250 miles apart. On several occasions, we were running on gasoline fumes before we found the next gas station. When we stopped for the night, it was always at one of the British Columbian campgrounds, which were always clean and well maintained. We even met some of the Royal Canadian Mounted Police. It took us fifteen days to travel the length of the gravel Alaskan highway.

We finally arrived at Eielson Air Force Base, which was twenty-two miles south of Fairbanks, Alaska, and at that time, the population of Fairbanks was around 1,400 people, with no fast-food restaurants or department stores.

I was assigned to the headquarters of the air force support group in an administrative position. After a while, I became tired of administrative work, and I cross-trained as a legal technician, which had an AFSC (air force specialty code) of 70550. I departed for Keesler Air Force Base, which was located in Biloxi, Mississippi. During the next eight weeks, I learned military law, civil law, and became a qualified air force court reporter, a skill that was needed for all court-martial charges, which were caused mostly by alcohol, drug, and spousal abuse. After the legal school, I returned to Eielson Air Force Base and went to work at the Base Legal Office Building, which we shared with the officers of special investigation (OSI), which is nothing more than air force plainclothes police. The air force dopers used to hang out by the outdoor OSI incinerator because once monthly marijuana was disposed of (burned).

One day I was running in the base field house (gym) and the airman in front of me just collapsed in midstride. We later found out he died of a massive heart attack.

While at work one day in the spring of 1974, one of the sergeants from the air force cold-weather survival school (cool school) stopped at our office, asking for volunteers to help find a missing Department of Defense (DOD) civilian. I volunteered and found myself in a boat in the middle of one of the lakes on Eielson Air Force Base throwing and retrieving a grappling hook. On the second throw, I was pulling the grappling hook toward the boat when the hook snagged something heavy. As I continued to pull the grappling hook in, I could see that there was a man attached. I finally got the grappling hook up to the boat, and the man's head broke water. He was dead, his skin was pale white, and his eyes were open with his glasses still on his face.

While I was stationed at Eielson Air Force Base, we had fifteen people killed over a five-year period, not including the loss of an Air Force RC707, which was a reconnaissance aircraft flying over the Bering Sea, very close to the Russian territory. We think it was shot down by Russian fighter planes, with all hands lost. The plane's code name was Amber. After Amber went down, we renamed our field house Amber Hall in honor of the lost crew.

I did a lot of hunting and fishing in Alaska. I even learned to reload ammunition for my Winchester Model 70 300 magnum, with which I killed an 1,800-pound, two-year-old moose. I also killed five caribous and one very mean wolverine. The moose shot was at 600 yards running and the wolverine was at 175 yards.

We had a bunch of remote early warning radar sites. The most notable was the Indian Mountain site that had three levels. One year, I think it was in 1973, the upper site at Indian Mountain froze up solid, and the crew had to move down to the second level. A few days later, the second level froze, and the crew moved down to the first level. That site also froze solid, and we sent in a C-130 to evacuate the radar crew because it just kept getting colder and eventually reached a mean temperature of eighty degrees below zero, where it stayed for two weeks.

It was so cold that year that our coal-fire base heating system broke down because the huge piles of coal froze solid. All hands, officers, and enlisted alike were called on to hand-shovel coal for the heating system. If we had not shoveled the coal by hand, the entire base would have frozen solid, and we would have been forced to evacuate everyone stationed at Eielson Air Force Base.

I remember the two-week cold spell in the last part of December of 1973. On December 30, I took my wife Sally out for our anniversary dinner, and when we arrived at the steak house, I let the engine of our Ford Pinto run because it was eighty degrees below zero. Wefinished dinner, and when we went out to our car, it was still running but not very well because the exhaust pipe was freezing closed even with the engine running, so I knocked the ice out of the exhaust pipe, and we started back to the base, which was about five miles away. When we started moving, the flat spot, which a car gets when stopped, remained flat for at least three of the five miles. It seemed as though our tires were square instead of round, which resulted in a teeth-chattering drive back to base.

I kept extending my tour in Alaska until we had been stationed at Eielson Air Force Base for five years. Regulations would not permit us to stay any longer, so I volunteered for a tour at Francis E. Warren Air Force Base in Cheyenne, Wyoming, which was approved by air force headquarters. We departed Eielson Air Force Base in May of 1975. We had decided to take the inland ferry from Haines, Alaska, to Prince Rupert, British Columbia, but we first had to drive through the Yukon, which took us through Haines Junction and on to Haines, Alaska. I remember driving down this one-lane frozen road and looking up at snow on each side of the road that had to be at least thirty feet deep because they had thirty-to-forty-foot lodge pole pine trees along each side of the frozen road to guide the snow plows.

We finally arrived at Haines, Alaska, and drove our car on to the ship. Then we had a beautiful trip to Prince Rupert, British Columbia, seeing killer whales, glaciers, and some of the most spectacular scenery on this world.

I drove the car off the ship, and we started the long drive down through British Columbia and on to Cheyenne, Wyoming, going through Washington State, Idaho, and Montana before we finally arrived at our first destination, which was Francis E. Warren Air Force Base in Cheyenne. On the first leg of the drive, I had to take over the driving because my wife has a tendency to fall asleep at the wheel on long trips. We stopped at Cheyenne to check in to my new assignment. Then we continued on to my wife's home in Chicago, Illinois. Then we drove to Reston, Virginia, where we visited with her dad, Jim Vogel. Then we went on to Louisville, Kentucky, to visit my family. We returned to Cheyenne and to the legal office at Francis E. Warren Air Force Base where I took over the as a noncommissioned officer in charge (NCOIC). The legal office was a disaster because the acting NCOIC had not filed any of the air force regulations, nor did he keep the law library up-to-date. For three or four months, I was working twelve hours a day, six days a week, and even bringing home work each night, which my wife helped me with. We averaged about four court-martials a month, plus about one hundred to one hundred fifteen Article 15s, which is nonjudicial punishment for minor offenses. We also had AFM 39-10 and AFM 39-12 discharge, which were deemed for the good of the air force.

I was NCOIC from 1975 to 1982, and then I retired. I choose not to test for master sergeant because the promotion would have required me to serve an additional two years and, most likely, a transfer to another base, so I took my retirement discharge in December of 1982 and went to work as a security guard/bouncer at the Little America Resort Hotel in Cheyenne.

Heimlich Procedure

We bought a house in 1980 and moved from Francis E. Warren Air Force Base. One night, after I retired from the military, we were eating dinner, and my wife choked on some food. She was not breathing. I got behind her and performed the Heimlich procedure, which dislodged the food from her throat, and she started breathing again. About a week later, the same thing happened to my youngest son Ed, and I again performed the Heimlich procedure, dislodging the food and restoring his breathing. After these two events happened, I personally thought that God and Satan were involved—God helping me save my wife and son and Satan trying to kill them.

I worked at Little America for about three months before I was selected for a temporary position at the Bureau of Land Management (BLM), which is a federal branch. I learned that a woman who worked for the Forest Service had sued the Forest Service and the Department of Agriculture for sexual discrimination and had won her case in the federal district court. The federal judge decreed that the federal civilian workforce would be composed of 50% white males, 47% women, and 3%

minority, which, in fact, set federal job quotas, which would not have been too bad, except that the quotas were averaged bureau-wide. The Bureau of Land Management in Cheyenne, Wyoming, was composed of 90% women, and because of the bureau-wide quota averages, a white male working for the Bureau of Land Management had *no chance* for promotion. The job I had, which was collecting the legal land descriptions for the entire state of Wyoming and also the land status from documents and master title plats, as well as Indian documents, was at a GS-10 or GS-11 grade, and I could never get above a GS-5, step 10.

I did see my son, Jimmy, and daughter, Belinda, again until 1988 when I went home to see my mother. I arrived one day, and my sister Carolyn and I went to see Mom in the nursing home that night. The next morning, while staying at the house of my stepbrother Bill, I got a call from my sister that Mom had died in her sleep. Mom's death was listed in the *Louisville Courier-Journal* newspaper. The wife of my son, Jimmy, read about her death and told him. Jimmy then called me at Bill's house and asked if he could visit with me. He wanted to bring his wife and twin boys (my grandsons). Of course, I said yes because I had always loved them. It was a nice reunion, except that I was unknowingly suffering from deep depression from my Vietnam combat tour. Jimmy told me he didn't see how I could not be excited seeing him and his family after all those years. The answer was I was sick from Vietnam combat with postcombat, delayed posttraumatic stress disorder (PTSD). That night Jimmy picked up my daughter, his sister Belinda, and we all went out to dinner at a fancy restaurant. Jimmy asked me what

I wanted to drink, and I told him coffee. He then asked me if I had stopped drinking alcohol, and I told him yes, I had.

During my stay in Louisville, my daughter, Belinda, invited me and my sister Carolyn over to her house one night, and while we were talking, she asked me how could I have stayed married to my present wife, Sally, for so many years and why didn't I stay with Carolyn, her mother. I told her that people change and situations also change, which was not what she wanted to hear. While we were talking, her mother, Carolyn, called on the phone. When Belinda told her that I was sitting there in front of her, Carolyn told Belinda to ask me if I would go out with her for a drink (alcohol). I told her no and that I didn't drink anymore. I also told her I was remarried to a great woman.

My daughter belonged to a Southern Baptist church, and my sister Carolyn told me that I should call Belinda to see if we could all go to church together that weekend before my return to Cheyenne, Wyoming. To my surprise, my daughter said yes; so on Sunday morning, Carolyn and I picked Belinda up, and we went to church. It was the first time I had been in a church in years. Toward the end of the service, the minister told everyone to shake hands with the people around them. I turned to Belinda, and she threw her arms around my neck and said, "I am so glad you came home, so glad you came to see us, and I am so glad you are here in church with me now." That was the last time I would ever see my only daughter or my granddaughter JulieAnn, that beautiful Sunday in 1988.

In October of 1996, I had a nervous breakdown, which was caused in part by the job discrimination at the Bureau of Land Management. My wife finally convinced me to seek medical help from the Veterans Administration Hospital in Cheyenne. I had just shut down, both mentally and physically, and had not slept for three months because my Vietnam nightmares were so bad. Before going to the VA Hospital, I typed all my symptoms down. When the psychiatrist read them and had evaluated me, she said I had a classic case of postcombat delayed posttraumatic stress syndrome and immediately got me classified as disability, "service-connected." She put me on antidepressants, and I also went to a Vietnam veterans PTSD workshop, which consisted of therapy and anger management workshops, at the Veterans Administration Hospital in Denver, Colorado.

I went back to work in January 1997, and I told the BLM management that if I was not given a promotion at once, I would put in my retirement paper and retire in June of 1997, which I did because there was no way I would be promoted.

After I retired, I worked at several part-time jobs but had to stop working entirely because I had to take care of my grandson Chuck Detheridge. My son Edward and my daughter-in-law Edna separated and divorced because Edward abused Chuck and Edna verbally and physically. About May of 2005, I was taking care of Chuck while his mother Edna worked.

I have been back from Vietnam for thirty-eight years, and I still have flashbacks of incidents/battles in Vietnam, as well as nightmares. It seems as though part of me was left behind in Vietnam, never to return and make me a whole person again, because of the battles I participated in and the horrible things that I witnessed. It is almost like Vietnam burned a permanent hole in my very own soul. I can only hope that God will forgive me for the things I did in the Land That God forgot—Vietnam.

I am now seventy years old and have 60% Vietnam Combat Disability, Air Force Retirement, Bureau of Land Management Retirement, as well as Social Security Retirement. Even with four retirements, my wife and I have trouble making ends meet.

I figure I may have ten to twenty years of life remaining to be with my wife and loved ones, and after that, who knows?

My life, at first, was pretty worthless and bad, and I didn't get any better until I met and married my wife, Sally, but it would take a combat tour in Vietnam to really make me grow up and become a man who haven't had a drink of anything stronger than a Coca-Cola for thirty-eight years.

I didn't ask to be born, but I finally realized that I would just have to start making the right choices, and my life would eventually become better as I grew older.

When my sister Carolyn was born in August of 1953, we were all so happy to have her in the family. I never did get to know her because I was enlisted in the regular US Army in 1962 when she was only eight years old. I had not been back to Louisville since our mother died in 1988. My sister came to visit my family and me twice in Cheyenne, Wyoming, the first time in 1995, then again in 1999, when she and her third husband had separated and she filed for divorce. We had talked for a couple of years about my homecoming to Louisville for a visit.

Finally, in September 2004, I made the trip back home to Louisville, Kentucky. Carolyn and I had two very wonderful weeks together. After all the years that had passed, we finally got to know each other at last. We visited so many historical places in Kentucky that during my youth, I was always too busy to explore the beauty of my own state. We even went to Iroquois

Park, where I had spent a lot of time during my teenage years. The road leading to the lookout on top of Iroquois Hill was blocked off because of people dealing drugs, so my sister and I hiked to the top, which made me breathe a little hard, but it was so much fun making the climb and seeing the lookouts again that I had frequented as a teenager with some of my girlfriends. During these two weeks, I found out that my sister Carolyn is a truly wonderful person and that we have a lot in common, even our love of dark chocolate, which we never knew before. I finally got the chance to realize the love I have for my sister Carolyn, and that love grows stronger every day.

On my trip to Louisville in 2004, my sister called my son by my first marriage, Jimmy, and told him I was visiting from Wyoming. Jimmy came over to see us. Ironically, he only lived approximately one mile from my sister's apartment. I didn't see him again until the day I was to return to Wyoming. Jimmy knocked on the door, and I opened it because my sister was out, and to my surprise, he had his twin sons with him, whom I had not seen since 1988 when they were five years old. The boys had a lot of questions about my life and also about Vietnam and what I had done there. They were also curious, according to Jimmy, to know if I was bald. I talked with them and found out they had their own construction businesses. They also each had Corvette sports cars. (Maybe they take after their grandfather?)

In retrospect, if I had my life to live over, I would have shipped over to regular marine corps and never have gotten married. I really believe if I had become a regular marine and made the marine corps my career, I would have been killed in Vietnam. Why do I say I would have been killed in the marine corps in Vietnam? It is because I have very explicit nightmares of myself in marine corps jungle fatigues being shot at night in Vietnam; it's nighttime in almost all my nightmares. I don't know if the different life I may have had would have been any better. One thing I have learned is that every war is caused by politicians failing to talk/negotiate. When politicians stop talking, war starts, such as the unnecessary and unwinnable war in Iraq, which is both political and vindictive (George W. Bush), trying to finish the Iraq war of 1991.

Because of my PTSD, nightmares, and depression, I have a survivor syndrome, which is why I did live through Vietnam while so many of my fellow troopers did not. On occasions, I view and review the Christmas classic movie *It's a Wonderful Life* on VHS, trying to determine if my surviving the Vietnam combat made a difference. Is the world a better place for my having lived through Vietnam, or did my survival make a difference at all? I have been blessed by the birth of my grandson Charles "Chuck" Detheridge, and it has been a joy taking care of him, helping him prepare for adult life in the world and watching him grow into a fine young man.

I was blessed with another very wonderful grandson, Ryan James Detheridge, born to my son, James, and his lovely wife, Janay, on November 8, 2006. My wife and I have had the wonderful privilege of taking care of Ryan since he was about six months old. Ryan is wonderful, happy, and handsome who, I am sure, will grow into a fine, intelligent man. All in all, I think my survival of Vietnam and my long life has been a positive thing because of my wonderful wife Sally, my children, and my two wonderful grandsons, who I am sure will make a more positive contribution to the world than I was ever able to do. Thank you, God, for loving me in spite of myself!

My wife, Sally, decided to stop taking care of our grandson Ryan because she just didn't have the energy anymore. We lived our lives trying to stay busy, but the only thing we ever did was go out to eat. Sally started telling me of these health problems she was having, and her health became so bad in December of 2011.

Right after Christmas, Sally got to the point where she couldn't breathe. Prior to Sally's problem, I was diagnosed with melanoma and was operated on by a Veterans Administration surgeon. He told me he couldn't get all the cancer out, so I was operated on again by a local woman surgeon. Six years have passed and I have continuously monitored for recurrence of the melanoma with negative symptoms so far.

In January of 2012, Sally got to the point where she could not breathe, so I took her to the Cheyenne Medical Center, and they began running tests on her to determine her medical problem. They took a biopsy and sent it to a lab in Denver, but they were unable to identify what type cancer she had. Sally's oncologist sent another biopsy to the Mayo Clinic, and after three weeks, they identified her cancer as T-cell leukemia, a disease no one had previously survived before. The doctors started treating her with the most powerful drugs available.

Sally was in and out of the hospital for over a year, and then in the spring, in March 23, 2013, the angels came to the Cheyenne Hospice Center and took her to our Lord in heaven.

WRITER'S NOTE: I recently asked my grandson Chuck what he thought was the most thankless but most honorable/

important profession a man could devote his life to. His reply was policeman, fireman, or doctor. I told him they were all honorable and important jobs, but I truly believe that the most thankless and honorable profession is to devote one's life to the military service of a man's country. I say "thankless" because the general consensus of the American people to our military is to take us for granted and send us in harm's way when it is necessary to defend our country. We in the military are not appreciated until an aggressive foreign power becomes so strong that our country is in danger of being directly attacked and overran and the individual American has a very good chance of becoming a casualty in a war on our own soil. Then the military, who sacrifice their life daily, are then appreciated.

I am older now and starting to realize my mortality. It is no fun when a person's body starts to fail him in some ways and the mind is still sharp.

Jim Mulloy, my friend of sixty years, who I served with in the Marine Corps was mute for over a month and I was worried about him, but I received a message today telling me he had an operation to insert heart stints and is trying to recuperate. This makes me sad because he just turned eighty-five; he's two years older than me. But as a friend once said, we have had our time in the sun. It's time to move on, so I have done my best at this life and hope God can forgive us for what we have done in war as well as in life.

Semper Fidelis 'til I die.

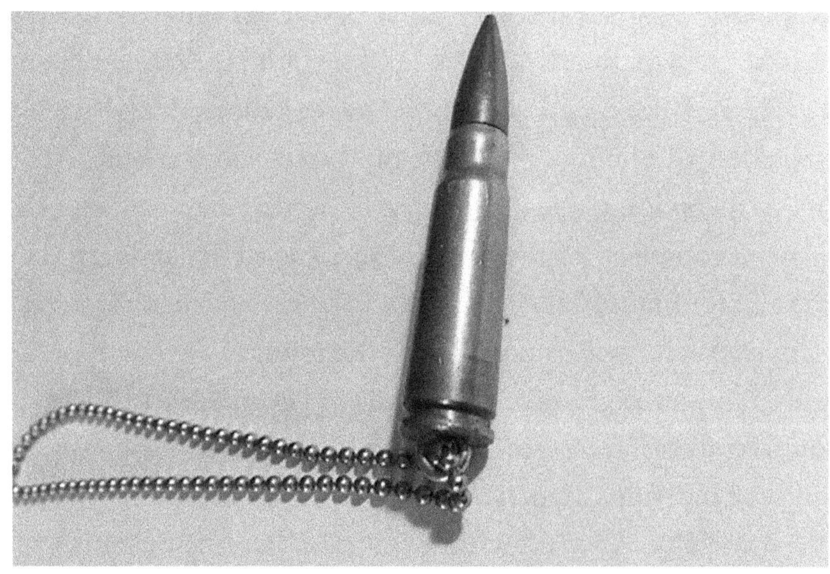

A 7.62mmx39mm used by the North Vietnamese Army against us in the Vietnam War fired in the AK47 Russian rifle

A1E Sky raider of 1st Air Commando Squadron Bein Thuy, Vietnam

Along the Bassack River which runs into the big Mekong River

Army Catholic Chaplain with homeless street kids in Can Tho 1966

Author after heavy weightlifting session

Army pilot with pet monkey

Author in Cheyenne, Wyoming

Author and sister in Laramie, Wyoming

Author and sister Carolyn during last visit
to Louisville, Kentucky in 2004

Author by Vietnamese guard shack

Author in front of LST ship on Bassack River

Author in Army 1963 45th Artillery Brigade

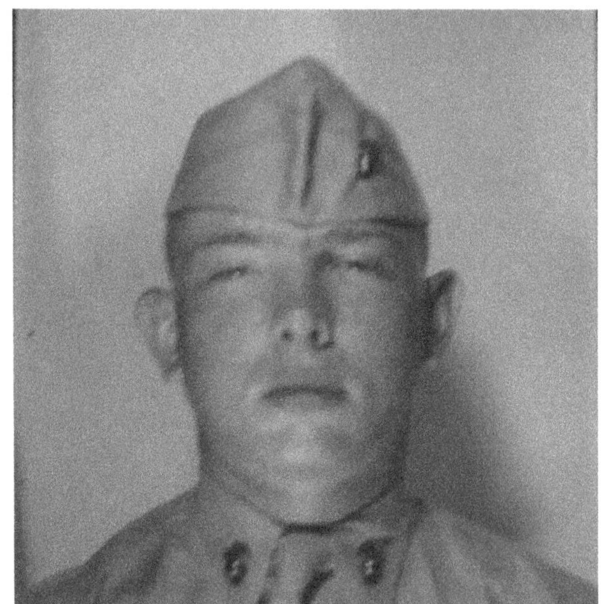

Author in Marine Corps

Author enjoying some free time in Can Tho

Author in Sacramento, CA prior to shipping out to Vietnam in 1966

Author on right in Lompoc, CA with friend

Author on Alaskan bear hunt 1973

Author on his Harley stroker motorcycle

Author with friend at Cam Rahn Bay, Vietnam 1967

Author with composite photos my sister sent me for Christmas

Author with GED from the Army

Author with Vietnamese hootch maid Cam Rahn Bay

Author's Marine Corps Cave with some of my drawings

Author with Vietnamese water boy who delivered water to us

Can Tho City with Bassack River in background

Can Tho with military vehicles in town square

Caribou and Puff The Magic Dragon aircraft at Bein Thuy

Flightline showing Caribou and C130 aircraft Bein Thuy

Civil war sharpshooter

Doc Halliday

Drawing of author at 19 years in Marine Corps

Drawing of Colonel Puller in Korean war 1950

Drawing of Marine mascot Devil Dog

Drawing of shooter in sitting position

Drawing of Wild Bill Hickok

Gunny Sergeant Carlos Hatchcock of "Marine Sniper" fame with 93 confirmed kills

My drawing of 2d Lt Chesty Puller in Nicaragua in 1926. The most decorated Marine in history of the Corps with 5 Navy Crosses

Old patriotic veteran saluting our colors

Rodeo cowboy

Special Operations troop firing his weapon offhand

Veteran saluting the colors

Woman firing gun offhand

James Bennett formerly James Robert Detheridge Jr

Guard duty with Army in 1966 Can Tho, Vietnam

ANNIVERSARY SECTION INSIDE

A 28-page special section inside today's Wyoming Tribune Eagle covers the Pearl Harbor attack minute by minute, how the United States mobilized after the attack, what Christmas was like in 1941 and what life was like in the early 1940s. The section even includes a quiz so you can test your knowledge.

REMEMBERING

PEARL HARBOR

"I WAS ... A SAILOR DOING MY JOB"

94, of Cheyenne will be a guest of honor tonight at a Pearl Harbor remembrance dinner at First Chris

My good friend Rowland Thomas who was at Pearl Harbor when bombed by the Japanese

Old veteran in uniform saluting colors

Saigon, Vietnam

Waterfront market on the Bassack River Can Tho, Vietnam

Mama Saun at river market

Picture of Vietnam Wall with spirits of fallen troopers appearing

This is Bach a 14 year old boysahn who saved the authors life in 1966

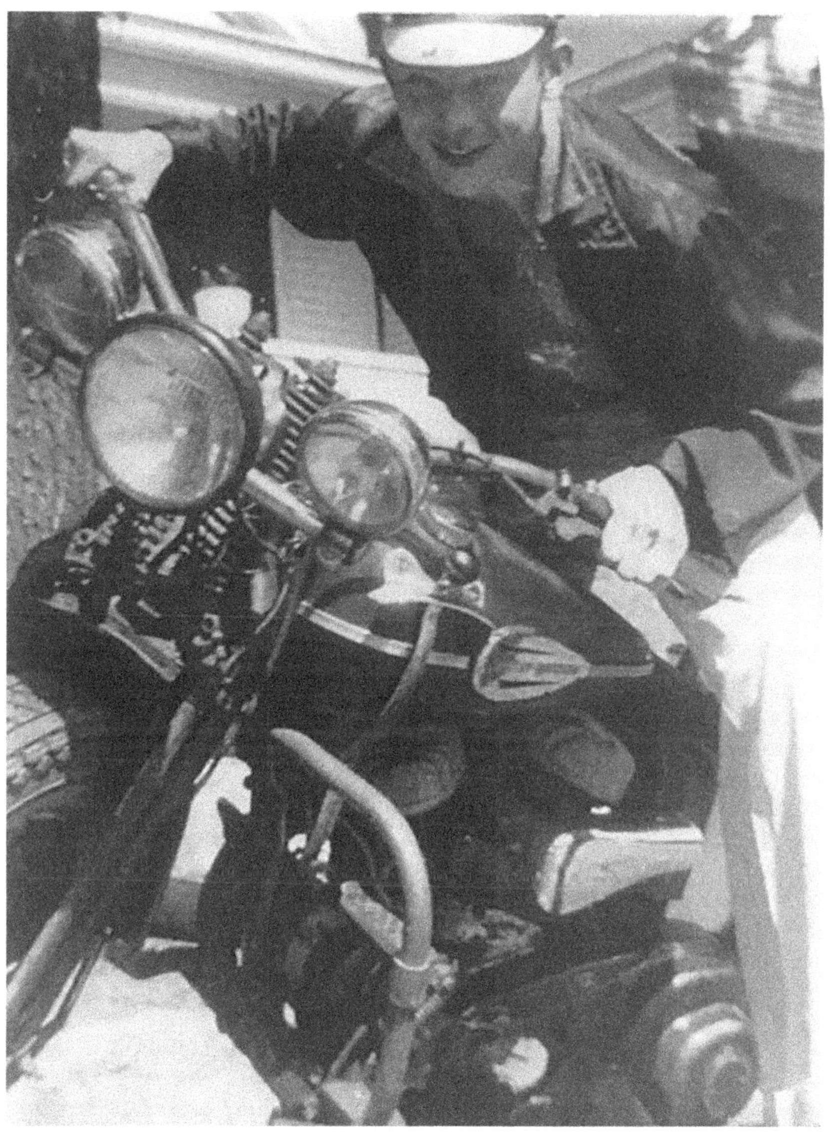

Riding my Harley 45 cubic inch with hand shift

The most beautiful photo of the Vietnam Wall

CPSIA information can be obtained
at www.ICGtesting.com
Printed in the USA
BVHW081531140119
537772BV00008B/1145/P

9 781643 452821